GOD IS FOREVER BEGINNING

Seeing this truth through the eyes of a poet

By

Sarah Laymon Hallstrand

Dedication

This book is dedicated to my three granddaughters
Ingrid Margaret – Miriam Sarah – Rosemary Schuyler

Each One, God's New Beginning

Acknowledgment

How does one express enough appreciation for all the people who have touched my soul with encouragement? My father, Charles Laymon, was an author and professor having written thirteen books on the life and teachings of Jesus for the United Methodist publishing house of the denomination. Growing up, he encouraged me to open my eyes to the wonders of our world. My mother was a social activist in her quiet way. They both had a profound influence on my life.

My husband John, the love of my life, has stood by me offering his support for my ministries in the local church as well as denominational leadership for fifty years in our marriage. His professional world centered on mainframe computer technology as an application software developer. As a couple we are different as we are the same. I value his thoughts and hugs of encouragement.

I have learned so much from the Lively Literary Ladies of Presbyterian Village. We write and share our creations with each other. Sometimes we enjoy "belly laughs" or sympathetic tears, but always tea is served at our monthly gathering!

Special friendships with people who live far away but have always been available for a chat or a prayer by phone are Evelyn Brown and Virginia Reed. These friendships were forged in the eighties and nineties and their encouragement helped me believe in myself as a writer.

Our daughter, Lillian, is a busy mother of three daughters, a third generation minister, as she speaks of her calling, loving wife to a successful Oncologist, community leader and active in her national sorority gave a final admonition to me, "Mom, just do it"! I did just that.

May these poems speak to your heart.

Meet the Author

Speaking of *New Beginnings*, I have had a few that led to the writing this book. I value my ordination with The American Baptist Churches and title, "Reverend". Later, I felt the need to improve my consulting skills and went on to earn a Doctorate in Ministry and later a Certified Financial Planner designation to add value to my ministry with clergy families.

Although preaching and consulting were satisfying work, nothing compares with the joy pondering and writing brings to my spirit. These poems are Holy conversations with God. I pray that they will be meaningful to you, also.

Blessings,
Reverend Doctor Sarah Laymon Hallstrand

Table of Contents

A Love Well Lived

diamond under the tree
May I have this life?
I love you and you love me
one life for two hearts

ministers at the altar
Love is spirit led
we sealed our pledges with vows
upon holy ground

promises made
Loved ones stood by us
smiles spread out on their faces
we kissed "for good luck"

honeymoon time
We held hands with glee
shining brightly in our smiles
we have just begun

like fine wine
Time is on our side
year after year is a gift
we are still learning

tough love
Our lessons are hard
patience and forgiveness too
like glue they bind us

for all eternity
A love that lives on
a friendship too strong to die
as a shooting star

Happy Anniversary, John

A Matter of Time

Before dawn, it took me on a walk through a patch of woods. A miniature forest of tall oaks and wide maples. Tucked among them were slender birches and willowy shrubs. This chill in the air began to blow harder against me. I lowered my head as to push against this invisible power. I shivered from its blow. Something called me to lift my head and open my eyes wide.

What I saw took my breath, as there in the blue inky sky of autumn rose the refreshed sun yawning at this break of dawn. This bright warming sight on a November morn welcomed me as a witness to this annual shedding for winter.

Another strong gusty blow must certainly know my desire for change. Once falling dry dusty leaves spinning and flipping on their journey caught my attention. Today, I have eyes only for falling crystals that dance in the air as little unique mirrors of rainbows. Moist frozen tears of delight will come to cover this dry fading brown and gold. I welcome this new season when nature becomes a magical fairyland of colors and sounds playing upon the snowy soft pillow of Winter.

But I must ask, "Why do you make me wait?" I just know that my question burst forth from my anxious inner child. I know the time had not yet fully arrived in North Georgia. It will snow in due time. Wait, watch and feel the damp chill in the air. Something is coming.

A Summer Visit

I took a leave of absence from my old tree friends along the creek
As time went by, my heart grew lonely for their chatty
conversation
Alas, their once chattering boughs now were limp and their voices
weak
The summer sun's heat stilled their leafy chatter but not my
expectation
Soon the sun changed position and the evening breezes returned to
fan
Aloft on cool breezes we whisper sweet nothings as if we just
begun

Along Came July

The pink myrtle blooms
appear floating in a tree
magical surprise!

How can this be true?
my eyes do not deceive me
they are nestled there

Your eyes do not lie
"yes" and "no" to that notion
mystery rules thoughts

So be it for now
humor is appropriate
listen to me laugh

Something fun and true
fills my soul with joyful glee
it dances to it

God knows I need it
the world has trash and treasures
turn on your heart-light

Beauty everywhere
God is in us to restore
blemishes removed

Let's get busy now
nature cannot wait longer
commitment bears fruit

Anchors Aweigh!

My heart is burdened
it is anchored in darkness
madness is crazy

Youth murder others
others take aim on the young
will the old be next?

This is nonsensical
we are down the rabbit hole
life is living hell

A raging tempest
anger swirls inside our cup
mad hatters we are

What now shall we say?
"off with their heads" heartless queen
pain begets more pain

Climb out of this hole
seek our better angels' help
take the high road now

You know what to do
so why do you make us wait?
more will die or cry

Pull up your anchor
cast off to healing waters
each one lend a hand

Autumn Leaves

Nature has a heart
that beats the seasons of change
from bright green to orange

Like a clock moves
its hands to be read as time
so trees tell us when

We are like the leaves
that are nurtured by their tree
season to season

The branch is our home
our stem clings to it for life
we draw sustenance

Rain and sun they need
like kisses and hugs each day
are good for our soul

I see the changes
and note their uniqueness too
yellow turns to brown

Some around their edge
highlighting their shape and size
some speckle with flecks

Some leaves just turn brown
In a hurry for release
strong winds they await

So we also change
each in their own way and time
their truth and grace show

May our stems hold on
for many wonderful seasons
our lives bright with love

Be Bop'n Robin

Such a happy bird is the red Robin
His head does bobble with every wobble
His sights set on the wormy ground
As his beak turns up and over what lays around
My gaze is transfixed on his swagger
As with every worm he gets fatter
King of the flock, the best of the tweeting lot
Because the Robin heralds the arrival of Spring

I wake to the noisy twittering of birds
Wondering what time is it?
A loud impatient song sings out
"Spring has come a calling"
"Tis time to get up you sleepy head"
This nagging bird chirps without ceasing
"Get up, get out of bed 'cause the sun is red
Live, love, laugh and be happy"

"How come that Robin is so happy?"
"Why he's got hope in his heart."
Poking under a leaf might turn up a juicy prize.
So, I better get my swagger going
Maybe I'll turn up a hidden glorious day
To live, love, laugh and be happy!

Body And Spirit A Reunion

Sometimes age marks us
Lines playfully cross the face
Making deep wrinkles

My heart sees our youth
Good times we had together
Fate took us Northward

Students and training
Different callings for each
Boston is our root

Many years apart
Never forgotten friendship
We are together

Time will write our song
The best is coming our way
We shall sing and dance

The stars are telling
The rest of our friendship tale
Never ending love

Canadian Maritimes Cruise

Boston before the cruise was this happy reunion of my best friend of my high school and college years. Sixty-Two years of friendship with almost all of it at a distance. It is amazing how much we recall about our times together and the unexpected joy of being in Boston after college for each of our advanced vocational studies. Nancy as a teacher and ministry preparation for me.

Clumsy

A PRAYER OF SUPPLICATION

I know...
You know...
Such weakness...
JESUS...
I confess...
Hurt...
Broken to the chase...
I stretch my throbbing limb…
In return to reveal...
Bandaged by Love…
Tears dry…
Here comes the sun.

COVID-19

In the beginning it was very quiet
Someone hit the pause button
Its April 2020 and the world is stirring once again
I sense we are coming to from a coma of fear
Here is the short of a very long story
A virus invades deep inside us
As a successful contagion, it can kill
Whatever the outcome, it always leaves a part of itself
Alas, this invisible germ gets a second chance
Until an antidote is discovered, we fight on
I don't think. I do feel.
Isolated and very vulnerable
I feel bored, fearful and angry all together at once
I am bereft of spirit, not myself
I try to imagine who I was before the virus
Particles of my life are magnetized by my emotions
Bits and pieces of me join together inside my bony spirit
What I felt was lost is found and miraculously made new
I see them! I hear their voices! I embrace them!
They are a welcomed community to my empty world
A smile crosses my face when I sense I am not forgotten
The deadly threat is passing over us
Celebrate this Passover!
The stone that separates us is rolling away
Celebrate this Easter!

Dreamer Dream On

In search for meaning
A class on dreaming
Table talk partner
Smiles with nervous eyes
Matching my own.
So we listen.
Words and drawings to
See the stuff of dreams.
Different sameness
Brings us together
She flying above it all
I speaking to it all
Wisdom's power reaching down to heal
Love's power reaching out to guide
Dreaming is God's desire for you
To be who you dream.

Dreaming is such a special gift, so I wonder if, in spirit form, I still will dream. Will I be able to make a dream for someone who can't dream? Perhaps I will give sweet dreams to those frozen in their nightmares. If in your dream you feel happy and blessed, then hold on to it. God is speaking.

Glimpses of Truth

I see her walking
gingerly taking small steps
so as not to trip.

Fall leaves are present
their bright colors lift my heart
but her head is bowed.

I ask myself why
she resists looking upward
is it fear or pain?

Her neck looks "frozen"
so tightly fused is the joint
that she cannot turn.

I see this clearly
as she sits down on a bench
to rest her body.

Aging is painful
as arthritis invades bones
God's Love helps us cope.

God sends her a leaf,
colorful shades of crimson,
lay upon her lap.

With bowed head she sees
the gifts that lay around us
a carpet of joy!

"Open my eyes that I may see. Glimpses of truth thou hast for me. Place in my hands the wonderful key. That shall unclasp and set me free."

Clara H. Scott, hymn lyrics for "Open My Eyes, That I May See"

Go Fetch

Fur baby, go get it!
lets play our game in the house
Where is your froggie?

I toss and she runs
but first trips over her own feet
slipping and sliding

She keeps up the pace
and returns the frog to me
wagging her tail too

Her growls tell me much
such as how happy she is
playing tug-a-war

Sometimes she stumbles
with head over wagging tail
and comes back for more

I know she loves this
she kisses me on the nose
she is my best pal

She is our baby
we adopted her on sight
God made her for us

Heartstrings

Someone is pulling
I can feel the vibration
why are they pulling?

Maybe they need me
or I have forgotten them
which is regretful.

Such shame makes me blush
so many people with needs
including myself.

The tug is stronger
something is amiss, I know
"speak up" I say, "speak".

Now I am afraid
who could possibly need me?
A stranger perhaps.

Unsure of my self
I ready my heart for pain
but I hope for joy.

What or who wants me,
"Green Door" what's your kept secret
from many years past?

I am surely blue
but I am also bright orange
so pull all my strings

At last, I see it
gently she brushes my legs
she needs a love hug

Lo and behold her
she is our own furry baby girl
Liesl is her name!

Hello...Goodbye

I am here now
Not sure how long I'll stay
Don't you see it is not up to me to say?

I live in a wobbling bubble of "has been"
Who can tell when it will pop?
Worn but not really shabby best describes us
Me and this little world of mine
No longer the pride of the South Land
We march to a more distant drummer
A salute to what little of that is left in us

Once we were dream weavers
Now we are dream eaters
Feasting on morsels of unspent energy
We bless each other with kindness
By words and actions we give what we need
Where competition once reigned we now make room
When memory fails we fill in the blanks
When one stumbles we all fall

This is the bubble I call "Grace Land"
I am here now
Not sure how long I'll stay

Reflecting on moving into a retirement community.

Here Comes The Wren

Here comes the wren
He goes where I dare not go
Sprightly he hops into the dark spaces on this bright morning
Hunger seeks out a spider or wriggly bug

Under the grill cover he vanishes
He shows no fear
Waiting and wondering, I watch for him
He reappears with a jaunty hop

There goes the wren
He went where I fear to go
There are dark crevices and spaces within my soul
What lies waiting to be found?

This morning I am full of worries. I am fearful of what I seem to be unable to control. Word of a friend's diagnosis of cancer, the dreary news about the stock market's relapse into double digit losses, my prayers for a pastorate, our financial needs, talk of war and all other such terrors are some of the dark shadows in my life. And besides all this, I am afraid of spiders. But behold this little rusty wren hops onto the external landscape. I wonder......

Could I enter my dark internal landscape and like the wren eagerly seek food; spiritual food, that is. Satisfaction might be in the form of answers or thoughts of better questions leading to an even deeper probing into life. God satisfies with both. God can feed my hunger even as I become more famished for God's truth.

But I am the spider I fear, also. I am my own problem. In order to satisfy my fears and longings, I must be willing to be gobbled up and lose myself to God's love which searches for me like the wren.

In A Twinkling Of An Eye

Rites of passages mark the heart beats of time
as flags upon the landscape of a soul.
God's purpose; our calling never revealed in a moment
but unfurled as curtain calls.

Each change a scene in your original composition
which you play upon a living stage.
Private thoughts and feelings are soliloquy
springing from whispered conversations of the heart.

Upon the edge of my seat I watch the action
and can hardly sit through the intermissions.
The drama plays upon my face bringing laughter and tears
as I watch you change in what seems a twinkling of an eye.

I love you dear daughter for all the times of your life!

(Leaving for college, Fall of 1997)

In The Roar of the Stillness

In the stillness of the night I hold you tight
My fluttering eyelids open to see you in the shadows
Looking for the vision that crept through my dream
Slipping through the shimmering haze of dozing
A word planted in my mind rooted itself in my heart
Strange this conversation, I feel what I cannot hear
I speak in colors and draw images that ask
Silence, who are you?
Who am I to you that I hold you so tight?
Listen. The sound of silence is Love
No small voice but a great whirlwind
My mismatched pieces of dreams draw together
Dreaming a conversation
"And the Lord answered (Job) out of the whirlwind..."
"Be still and know I am God"

Lately, I awaken in the night with a sense of Presence beside me in the dark. My heart pounds in awe of something great and loving. I have pondered who is my visitor and why am I visited? I do not have rational answers but my heart knows. I sleep in heavenly peace.

Ingrid's Birthday

Her birthday is now
April showers brought May blooms
She is budding too

When she goes to school
In the Fall she will be six
She will learn much more

She is very kind
Her friends like her very much
She makes them feel loved

She is liked by all
Her name means "beautiful one"
She likes to party

Her eyes shine so bright
Like candles in the dark night
Love makes her glow so

Happy birthday dear
Nana and Bumpa hug you
We love you always

Let It Be...So

Paul was troubled in mind and spirit.
In the dream he told his deceased mother his troubles.
Across the abyss of death, she spoke to his troubled heart.
Her message breathed comfort into him.
It was a burst of fresh air to his weary cells.
He could think fresh ideas.
The message so simple and complex.
Like a "Rubik's Cube" it is meant to keep you up at night.
Paul could not let the puzzle rest.
He wrote the lyrics for a song for the Beatles.
The solution was now given to the world.
I listened to it in 1970 when the record was released.
But I heard it for the first time 40 years later.
One day, as I doted on my worries, I started humming.
Puzzled, I finally connected the tune to it's lyrics.
Listen!
Your hopes and dreams are coming.
Let not your worries become a hazard to your wishful dreaming.
There is work to be done, and God is on your side.
An angel spoke to Mary, who was troubled.
She would bear the Hope of the World, can you imagine?
Angelic visitations cannot be pushed aside.
She answered, "Let it be" as you have said.
The power to change is believing that nothing is impossible.
You can make a difference for the better in human history.
The difference is believing that nothing is impossible with God.
Work out your passions with God's desire for all good outcomes.
Whispering words of wisdom, together, we will turn out right.
"Twill be in the valley of love and delight."

Liesl

"Little Miss Bright Eyes"
she focuses on my eyes
mine are fixed on hers

what are we thinking?
lets think about our dreaming
dreams reveal our needs

I agree with her
what are the most important?
friendship and caring

Liesl likes to kiss
she likes to be held in my arms
she feels special there

lets play together
I will throw the ball to you
chase and return it

but first lets cuddle
her warm body fits my lap
I really love her

together my friend
we play in God's universe
and love binds us there

Memorial Day

No longer a day
it grew into a weekend
a time to reflect

Why do we make wars?
What motivates us to fight?
Are we mean people?

Do good people fight?
For good causes they will fight
it is a "just" war

But war is still war
old men send young men to war
women join the fight

Children suffer too
they bleed and cry for parents
their homes are destroyed

Happens all the time
all it takes is one gunshot
no motive given

War is fought at home
all it takes is more anger
misunderstanding

Why do we feel this?
lack of trust is there also
perhaps we can change

Put away the guns
dry the tears from violence
love is here to stay

Memories

Today I am home
I know because I feel it
keenly in my heart

I see memories
happy moments shine brightly
sadness sheds its pale

They all surround me
the happy and the sadness
life is all of it

I take joy in it
I have lived "large" in my time
loving and angry

So why must it end?
this is a silly question
my heart will go on

I will always love
I will always shun evil
I am always home

Migrations

Look at me, stewing in my own emotional juices!

Such a steaming sight I am for watering eyes!

Never mind,

Those wacky warblers didn't notice me.

Behind my glass wall, I saw them twittering, toddling.

Such an irreverent duo.

Redstarts stopping for playful mischief.

Lackluster young Cardinals surround their irreverence.

"Redstarts, Redstarts, go away, come again some other day," they chant.

Refreshed and dry eyed, I smile.

God interrupts my depression when these little travelers stopped by. My office window allows me to look on to the evergreen cave within a row of bushes. Daily living more often needs a generous dose of smile than frown. Be careful not to make more of yourself or any given situation than God does. "Tears, tears, go away, come again some other day."

Miriam Sarah

As I held you, I whispered in your ear, "Miriam" - "Sarah"
Two strong women of the Bible, their names you bear
Honoring your birth, they danced upon the stars
Glad music lightened their feet to jump for joy
These two you should know
Miriam, God's freedom dancer and prophetess
Her voice gave hope for those in captivity
Out of Egypt to The Promised Land, they walked
Free from bondage, at last, Miriam led them in a dance
Sarah, fearless and faithful, obeyed God's Call
so that what appeared impossible became possible
Mother of nations and kings, a royal princess she is named
We share this special name, "Sarah."
Nana sees a curious yet knowing look in your eyes
What problem needs to be solved?
It takes courage to trust what appears impossible can be possible
Healer of the sick or restorer of lost hope
I celebrate God's love for you to make things right
I shall always be with you in the dance for joy!
Your Nana

Morning Shadows

Shiny looming black shadows hover over the seeds of life
Hunger drives their search for tiny delicacies with clumsy spiked
beaks With every swing of the head, seeds shower down upon the
garden floor Frightened smaller feathered ones perch or lay low in
peek-a-boo safety
And watch and wait for the end of this crowish impertinence,
Boredom moves the heavy flock on and little spirits lighten
"Ding dong, the wicked witch is gone"
What was meant to spoil a meal has become a feast
Eager little beaks gobble up the tiny seeds upon the ground
And with bobbled heads all join in a happy celebration.

We live in a world with black shadows in the form of terrorism hovering over our lives. What good might come from it? I know in my heart of hearts that this evil will be stopped in due time. The question I have is about now in the meantime. What blessings or good can shower upon our daily living which meet our needs and feed our souls? It seems to me that God often turns misfortune into fortune. Let us keep our eyes open, minds alert and hearts ready to receive some good news.

My Boat Sprung a Leak

Oh, I am not myself.
I feel so weak.
Like a feather, I swoon in the air.
Hands descend everywhere over, under, around me.
Into the cold I am stretchered and am whisked away.
My body is placed into more grabbing hands
Inserting needles and wrapping tape
Around the pricking pain I feel something icy meeting warm.
My thoughts….where are my thoughts?
Be still, I AM HERE.

Memory jumps up of another white coat moment
"Daddy, tell me a story."
Silly tale he told I do not remember but his voice comforts my fear
Nervously now I make small talk afraid to listen
To what condition my condition is in
I repeat words of comfort, FEAR NOT, IT IS I.

Upon this dizzy scare, I find my soul's balance.
For weeks I am not myself and in need of cures.
Medicine drips into my stream purifying my life source.
Assurances of love steady my frantic thoughts about the unknown
"I love you, dear" "We love you, mom" "I love you, Nana"
Names of endearment cheer my lonely state of mind
"Soul Sister" "Good Buddy" "Best-est Friend"
I Fear not because the great "I AM" is in this love

Remember the story of the disciples lost in the chaos of their boat
in the storm?
They feared that the One who commanded the winds and waves
had left them in dreaming.
Why would they think their Master had forsaken them to be
sucked down into the dark waters?
They forgot they are loved.

Nature's Praise

The gnats dance midair
They form a column that rises
Thanksgivings for heat

Dragons in the sky
Landing on petals so soft
Thanksgivings for blooms

Ruffles dance and fall
Trees shed their reddish colors
Happy Creator

Such a sparkling white
Crispy crunch as I walk on
Forgiven and restored

Seasons ever changing
God's Spirit never leaves us
Grace and Peace for all

Pachelbel's Cannon on Heartstrings

Sitting by the fire
Upon my heart; not a lyre
Strumming so gently
a song with longing so dire

I hear with my heart
The urgent call of the lark
Your hate will break you
Into tiny bits that spark

What restores us whole?
The healing is for your soul
That is sacred ground
We listen in its foxhole

The eyes tell us all
The ears hear about our fall
Upon crooked stalks
Memories help us recall

We were made to heal
Wounds of others to reveal
Fire that consumes us
With such searing pain we feel

Bring soothing waters
My peace inspiring daughters
For this is your march
Inspire this change that alters

God is with you
I am with you
All creation is with you
Shalom is in you

Politicians Pontificate

My thoughts are frozen
Stuck in the back of my mind
My tongue is heavy
I wish I could sing or hum

I do not want hate
It is ugly and stupid
It fouls the air we breathe in
And destroys the world

There are those who lead
Others straight to Hell and back
Elected leaders
Who sweat and drool nothingness

Chaos ordered cake
Let them eat their full of lies
My daffodils laugh
Truth beams all sunshine goodness

I vote for goodness
The world belongs to us now
Saviors are needed
We cannot shirk our duty

Heal the earth and air
Enable the poor to rise
Commit your whole heart
See opportunities grow

Be still and watchful
A new day is coming now
Be glad and rejoice
"I am doing a new thing"
(Isaiah 43:19)

Rosemary Schuyler

The first time I ever saw your face
I beheld a tiny rosebud tightly wound
ready to begin unfurling its hidden delights.
Yours is such a beautiful face woven by cherubs.
Using the best features of your parents
Your lineage shines through your smile.
Each one of us carries our past even as we create our future.
The first time I ever held you I glimpsed into your tomorrows.
Your eyes revealed a loving heart and a curious mind.
I sensed you are an "old soul" possessing wisdom.
Your eyes were tiny candles that made your sweet face glow
The first time you moved your mouth as to speak.
I saw visions of hope form upon your lips.
Your Nana is a hopeful dreamer and a loving heart
I seek the truth I speak.
Your world needs dreamers and lovers.
Where there is no hope, we cannot dream or love.
I hope for your generation a kinder and gentler spirit.
You will supply lots of energy to that end.
My loving spirit is with you, now and always.
Whenever you giggle, care for someone, or have an inspired idea,
Remember me and I will never forget you.

Sacred Friends

Forever my friend
I hold you dear to my heart
your wisdom I heed

You seek truth like me
we listen with kindred souls
our minds sharply honed

Together we learn
how to become more human
and feel as we think

The joy that we know
gives us hope for the future
some day we will see

God's total design
and know our place within it
what joy it will bring

Until then we play
in the universe we know
wish upon a star

Happily composed after my birthday celebration with friends.

Sea Me

She caught my fancy under the midnight moon, these
strung lantern lights streaming along its mast.
"Party hardy you ship of fools"
as you trip and slide high as a kite to the steady beat
of those blinking lights.
We slip and slide upon the waves together
this gypsy vessel and my ship The Silhouette.

I wonder if you wonder as we wander
On this wild foam of watery skin?
My thoughts ride upon the waves
until they dive into the ocean's depths
taking along my feelings.
Once upon a time, a salt dolly stood upon the beach.
She wondered what water felt like.
The waves invited her to get to know each other
So this brave doll jumped into the arms of a wave
Such a strange sensation she felt
to lose herself yet still sense herself
Lost and found, she exclaimed
The sea and me are one!

Pounding upon my shore are waves of knowing.
Salty tears for loss and still for joy.
To know, I must discover me
dissolving in the great sea of life.
Questions with Answers
Sea Me

So Strong and So Fair
Is My Granddaughter, Ingrid

Fluffy, the blanket rises and falls with her every breath
Sleepy head nestled against father's strong chest
Mesmerized, my eyes grasp this lovely scene
Anticipating a revelation, patience rewards
It is in her hands!
Her purpose reveals itself
On the one hand, her soft fingers clinch in a fist
Hold it tightly, Sweet One, for peace and goodness comes with a
price.
Be brave, little fist, and rail against the evils of this world.
On the other hand, I see it open and wide as if to bless and nurture.
Sweet One, you are possessed by these two narratives…
Be not afraid to stand against the wrong for what is right
Bless what comes from that struggle
Peace and Prosperity, fruit of the battle won
by the hands of beautiful Ingrid.

Soul Talk
(Granddaughter Ingrid)

Her face turned to mine
as our young and old souls sang
together with glee.

We greet the sunrise
and witness each sunset too
marking days passing.

These are special ones
learning to love our planet
as well as others.

We forget sometimes
our lessons about loving
others as our self.

When not at our best
we fail to love others too
and tears trickle down.

Tears wash away grief
as we ask for forgiveness
and we love again.

God is great and good
mighty deeds and loving heart
never to leave us.

God is forever
and will never leave your side
happy is this news!

Spring

such a drizzly day
fairy wings cannot fly now
butterflies are soaked

nothing but gray skies
but below there bursts color
Spring paints her pastels

purple, white and pink
are her favorite palette
sweet sight to enjoy

my heart laughs out loud
how crazy is that methinks
sodden laden butterflies

deep inside each branch
there bursts forth nature's template
a colored flower

laughter is silenced
by this awesome truth I see
God's love has a face

What is divine sees
nothing is ever hidden
Spring has met my need

Stormy Tango

Gracefully she moves
White crusted swells become swoons
Are caught in his arms

The sea is a dance
Moving together as one
Their embrace is tight

Watch the ocean age
Dark water turns foamy white
See these swells at play

Like bubbles bursting
Tiny rainbows rise above
With sun and water

The sea takes a breath
Tight foam turns to loose skin
A living being

Canadian Maritimes Cruise

Teardrops

Loveless and lonely, sad to say while
Clutching clothing, gritting teeth
Searing pain shoots another bolt of grieving
When will it stop?
Cries for help to those beyond me
My nerves are on fire and I grieve this loss
Body and soul are the same.

Aging plays its dirty tricks on my body
Messages misfire along frayed connections
Pain and anger replace stable affection
How to repair these backbones?

My lids close shut with fear and frustration
I pray to the light behind my lids
To saints, I call you to gather up my spirit and body
Holding me, I relax … sweet tears flow
Salty hot.

As pain lets lose it's grip I let fly a groan
It is over and it is good
This a foretaste of heaven
Never again to feel this heavy hurt
Body and Soul

Thanksgiving 2022

The table is set
savory sweet aromas
we say "thank you, God"

Ingrid bows her head
she holds hands with Miriam
and Rosemary too

Thanks for family
turkey and pies we enjoy
all this and much more

God is great and good
we thank God for this bounty
we shall help others

We learn from this meal
the meaning of love and care
we share this goodness

Amen

The Dogwood Tale

Like teardrops roll down
upon nature's own sad face
the dogwood blooms fall

The nail marks so clear
I see the old story told
of God's love for all

It is Good Friday
what was meant as punishment
has become God's Grace

Petals soft and white
carpet the dark forest floor
Now I see the way

Love is not easy
fairness is not natural
we must not give up

The dogwood tells us
the old story of Jesus
how love conquers hate

The Heart Knows

Who can tell me why my eyes are blind?
My eyelids are wide open, but I do not see.
Teardrops roll down my cheeks, but I do not feel.
Surely, this is the work of the heart to know what I cannot see.

Who can tell me why my ears are deaf?
My ears are wide open, but I do not hear.
Teardrops roll down my cheeks, but I do not feel.
Surely, this is the work of the heart to know what I cannot hear.

Who can tell me why I cannot speak?
My mouth opens, but I do not say.
Teardrops roll down my cheeks, but I do not feel.
Surely this is the work of the heart to know what I cannot say.

Stand before me eyes, ears and tongue to answer!
"It is your soul that sees, hears and speaks the truth in love.
Many see but do not behold,
Many hear but do not follow.
Many speak but do not persuade."

If this is a gift, why am I chosen?
If this is a curse, what have I done to deserve it?
Wait and see.
Wait and listen.
Wait and ask again.
Many are given sight, sound and voice.
Few ask for it.

The Queen's Design

The small web perfect
a true Michelangelo
is this wee spider

The canvas hanging
between wooden posts she draws
a circle of thread

Outer to inward
The silky design took form
she at the center

She wears only stripes
neon strips of color bright
she loves to attract

My attention caught
in her web I see beauty
but also danger

Winged creatures all small
fell prey in the nighttime dark
to the lure of her

Well nourished she grows
what a sight for September
as fatter she'll be

Her throne awaits her
The center she occupies
I bow to honor

The Time Has Come

Each one of us shines
and your sparkles excite me
together we glow

Do you see the dark?
Mystery thrives on it there
Who or what is it?

Whatever it is
we must attend to it now
before we are lost

Evil shuns the light
so we assume it is bad
but we could be wrong

Some of us are shy
and seek the cover of dark
why not shine on them?

I have light to spare
so do you have more to give
the source is our love

Lets ignite the world
with enough desire to change
for the good in all

Time's a wasting' fast
no more helter skelter craze
work plans for the dream

The Tip Of The Iceberg

I liken myself to the floating iceberg
as I move forward bobbing on the life giving and taking sea of
time
I am more than cells upon cells that grow and slough off
my sagging and wrinkly skin are mementos of my past
beauty is just something that can be peeled off the surface
but loveliness resides deep within my soul
forever creating from the inside outward
I bloom like the Iris bedded deep in the dark earth
nourished by the wisdom of the ages marked by seasons
from this darkness, I explode into the sunlight
my soft petals and crown of purples, pinks and yellows
greet the warm sunlight that calls me forth
I laugh at my foibles and slowness as I bless my stumbling
remnant from my youthful escapades
those were the good days, we thought they would never end
but life is even better seen from both sides now
we remember and in that moment we are allowed
to live it again as a blessing
once we saw ourselves in a mirror dimly
but with aged eyes we see the truth
that life never ends...it is always beginning
I invite you to ponder what new thing
calls forth for you to be and do
look beneath life's surface and embrace the rest of you
just under the tip of the iceberg.

Thoughts on a summer's Day

The times of our life
does anyone know our time?
How is it measured?

We act like we know
some save the best for our last
like jam spread on toast

Others just can't wait
high on youthful energy
like Hershey Syrup

The mellow middle
knows what does a body good
mind and spirit meld

Does anyone care?
Creator God surely knows
when we waste our time

Teardrops above fall
on our hearts making grief
appear on our lips

Make haste for the prize
live your time all ways always
loving is a joy

For such is your time
to help others find their joy
Live! Live! is your joy

Twirling Dancers

A dazzling display of twirling dancers
are these falling leaves in my woods
Be they Oak, Maple or Birch they spin
and weave a magical blanket for warmth
A shield against the rain and fading sun

Mimicking icy snow, their stiff crunch under foot
sounds like chatter, an invitation to talk
I ask, "How was your trip?"
Dazzling I should think from those heights
But perhaps it was a blast of wind
that brought you spinning straight onto a pile,
Oh such a pity to miss the dance

They reply, "Do not fret as there are those who cling."
Theirs is inner strength to stay longer
The young birds need leaf protection
from the keen eyes of winged predators

Dazzling dancers
Spinners
For all creation has a purpose

Ukraine Spring 2022

Listen
Listen to the beat of my heart.
Listen to the beat of bombs exploding.
Listen to the beat of tiny feet running to catch up.
Listen to the beat of bare feet black and bloody by rubble.
Listen to the beat of teardrops falling on dirty cheeks.
Where am I?
Burning what is sacred the acrid black smoke chokes me.
Who once wore that mangled body on the road?
I must move on without looking back.
Their high pitched cries fill my ears as I shake uncontrollably.
Help me! Help me!
Muted by my fear, they fall on my deaf ears.
I fall on my knees and lift my eyes looking for help.
Seeking a vision that once gave me peace.
Peace, you are so very beautiful to behold!
Like a diamond set on a promise band,
Peace showers us with rainbows.
War is dirty, lifeless and it stinks of rancid fear.
Peace is life giving and fearless.
Please, let's give it a chance.
I swear it is not too late!

Upon Dark Waters

I am letting the good ship *Silhouette* take me for a ride
upon the dark waters of this Caribbean night.
The full moon reflects the sun's earlier light of the day
upon my dark figure leaning over the balcony railing.
My ghostly silhouette is cast upon the water.
The ship's steel hull shudders as it slams into the tall waves.
In a flight of fantasy I dream of this ship as a gypsy lady
dressed in organza with colorful ruffles that flutter seductively
with every shake of her broad shoulders.
She speaks to those who bend their ear to listen.
She hears my whispered wishes for adventure and steers the
course.
Below the choppy surface of waves there is another world to
explore.
This water makes me thirst for the meaning of The Sea.
I remember the story of the salt doll who was also curious to know.
She once stood upon the sand and watched the waves
greet her with playful splashes upon the shore.
She wondered what it would feel like to play in the water
so she took tiny halting steps to the water's edge.
When the waves kissed her toes she giggled because it tickled.
Little bits of her fell into the water in this playful encounter.
As she dissolved, she understood what had been a mystery.
I look up at the moon thankful for this memory with its wisdom.
Life is full of mysteries and adventures that tease me like the
waves.
To let go of my fears and experience what life has to offer me.
To meet the new and encounter the unusual is why I travel tonight
upon dark waters.

The Voice

In the beginning, there was the Voice
"And God said..." and life became
In our beginning there was the Voice
"And God said...and we cried
Each with a voice never heard before upon the earth

Some time ago, there was again the Voice
Heard by hearts gone deaf by despair
"And Jesus said..." and hope was heard again
Some time ago, some found their own voice
"And Jesus called...," and they followed to the ends of the earth

These became companion voices of the Voice
Enthused, they eagerly spoke to the needs of others
Inspired, they uttered words of wisdom to the confused
Encouraged, they dared to speak for God against the wicked
When they spoke, all could hear the Voice

The Voice of God is timeless truth, but
In time, the companion voices faded upon the earth
Their voices now whisper of love and friendship in our ears
Beyond time, these have found a new voice
Of eternal praise in the choral Voice of God

Listen, listen well
The Voice is calling and will not be still
Hear your call and give expression to the voiceless
In this early journey for the sake of others
your special sound blending with celestial voices
In the great "AMEN"

WORDS WORDS WORDS and a few more words…

One of my favorite songs from a Broadway Play is "Happy Talk" from the hit musical SOUTH PACIFIC. It is sung by the warm, loving and comical character Bloody Mary to a sailor and his beautiful Polynesian girlfriend who are falling in love. She sings to them that it is important to talk so that they can create a dream for their life together. It is "happy" talk because it is about what each likes to do. Get to know each other and discover a beautiful dream of what is possible for them as a married couple. Bloody Mary sings, "If you don't have a dream then how are you going to have a dream come true."

Words are thoughts, so thoughts, especially those shared with special people in your life, are the foundation of wonderful dreams. Not every dream comes true, but if not dreamed in the first place, you'll never experience what might be possible. It is good to think deep thoughts and those daydreams just might be your ticket to a successful adventure.

I saw a poster a long time ago, in the Sixties, when I was in seminary at Boston University. Standing behind the impressive pulpit was a caricature of a minister dressed in robe and collar regalia preaching. The caption was "Words, Words, Words" and with what appeared as spittle on the corners of his mouth, he appeared mean and dangerous. I guessed the picture was saying that words can kill dreams as well as give life. Ever heard this description of a critical and mean comment by someone as that person having a "sharp tongue"? It is so important that you pause and think before speaking, especially if the comment is about an idea, thing, or relationship that is important to the other person.

I attended a church service today. It is summer, which signals a more casual approach to worship. It was very nice and a comfortable mood showed on the faces of the worshipers. As a contrast, it was interesting that the sermon was based on the story of Jesus returning to his hometown, Nazareth and the cool and hostile reception he received as he preached in the synagogue. These were his neighbors who rebuked him. They knew him as a young carpenter assistant to his father, Joseph, not as a rabbi or teacher and so they were taken back by his wisdom as he spoke about the meaning of Holy Scriptures. Sharp tongues wagging, they shouted at him and ran him out of the building. I did not hear any positive or critical remarks about the sermon or the service at the close, so I am led to believe that it did not matter much to anyone. Now, in fairness, there may have been members who later did ponder why it is that prophets are not welcomed, even in their home town. They may have thought about their own stories of returning home different from when they left. We do change, and we do grow up. There are those moments when the "new you" is intimidating to those who have established ideas of how things should work and are, as we say, "stuck in a rut!" Intimidating is a polite way to say that your beliefs are shocking! But I believe it is a good thing to be transparent about your core values. Those who are quiet do not necessarily have nothing to say.

What if present-day worshipers took the teachings of Jesus to heart and allowed ourselves to be radicalized into modern prophets? You know, those preachers whose tongues are on fire with the zeal of God's dreaming for a transformation from brokenness into wholeness for the world. Not just for some but for all. And what with all that happy talk of restoration the dream caught on in every heart and stimulated imagination of how it would be accomplished. I wish worship had more "happy talk" so that we could share and dream together. Whoever reads this, I hope you, like Mary, the mother of Jesus, listen and ponder in your heart what God wants you to do. Whatever it is, it has to be born of a dream that is shared with others.

Worship Cravings

Dry spirit tongue laps this
tiny moment splashed with cleansing truth
that divine love reaches across my despairing abyss by
touching God's finger tip to mine.
This shock treatment releases my power to believe again
"God is forever beginning"
(I thirst for that whispered conversation of the heart)

Under the Big Top I stand upon scattered sawdust
cut from my giant memories of living faith
There, alive with colorful yet sedated pomp and circumstance
the ringmaster bids me to pay attention to God's
thirst for my splashing life waters
"God is forever desiring"
(I and Thou thirst to be present)

The quiet knowing that we belong together
in our longings as Creator and creation
grows strong as a spiritual Redwood
Together we stand ready to be made into the sawdust
upon which prayerful pilgrims will stand and know that
"God is forever loving"
("Yea, the sturdy dreamers answered, to the death we follow thee")

"Writing beneath the Lines"
Divine Proposal

Come Holy Spirit
Perch upon my heart strings
Inspired words take shape
Windows to the inner world
That mirrors what's beyond
Grace